Future-Proof Your Designs

Mastering UI/UX Design for the Evolving Digital World

By
web Maverick

DEDICATION

To all the passionate coders and aspiring developers out there who want to take their design skills to the next level, this book is dedicated to you. May it serve as your ultimate resource and guide as you navigate the ever-changing landscape of web design. Keep pushing the boundaries and innovating with your design, and may you always stay ahead of the curve. This one's for you.

Sincerely,

Web Maverick

Table Of Contents:

<u>Chapter 1: Applications for Business Applications</u>

Business applications are software programs intended to assist organizations in performing specific tasks or resolving particular business challenges. These applications vary from basic tools like word processors and spreadsheets to more intricate systems like enterprise resource planning (ERP) software or customer relationship management (CRM) systems.

Productivity software falls under one common category of business applications, including tools like Microsoft Office or Google Workspace, aiding employees in creating documents, presentations, and spreadsheets.

Collaboration software, such as Slack or Microsoft Teams, is another type that enhances communication and teamwork among employees.

Moreover, businesses frequently utilize specialized applications customized to their industry, like accounting software, inventory management systems, or point-of-sale systems. These applications enable businesses to streamline operations, boost efficiency, make data-driven decisions, and ultimately achieve their objectives more effectively.

1.1. HUMAN-CENTERED DESIGN AND DESIGN THINKING:

Human-centered design and design thinking are approaches that prioritize the needs and experiences of people to create innovative solutions.

1.1.1 Human-Centered Design:

Focuses on understanding the needs, behaviors, and emotions of the end-users. Involves engaging with users throughout the design process to gather insights and feedback.

Emphasizes empathy for users to create products and services that resonate with them. Encourages iteration and prototyping to test ideas and refine solutions based on user feedback.

Aims to improve user satisfaction, usability, and overall experience with the final product or service.

1.1.2 Design Thinking:

- Involves a creative and iterative problem-solving approach.
- Consists of five stages: empathize, define, ideate, prototype, and test.
- Encourages multidisciplinary collaboration to bring diverse perspectives to the design process.
- Prioritizes experimentation and learning from failures to drive innovation. Focuses on understanding the root causes of problems and

designing holistic solutions that address user needs effectively.

In summary, both human-centered design and design thinking are user-centric approaches that aim to create meaningful and impactful solutions through empathy, creativity, and collaboration. By putting people at the center of the design process and embracing a mindset of continuous learning and improvement, designers can develop products and services that truly meet the needs and expectations of their target audience.

1.1.2 DEVELOPING A UI BUSINESS CASE

Developing a UI (User Interface) business case is crucial for successfully implementing design changes or new features in a product or service.

- **Identify Business Goals:** Understand the overarching objectives of the project and how the UI design can help achieve them.
- **User Research:** Conduct thorough research to understand the needs, preferences, and pain points of the target users.
- **Competitive Analysis:** Analyze the UI designs of competitors to identify best practices and areas for differentiation.
- **Define Key Metrics:** Establish measurable KPIs (Key Performance Indicators) to track the success of the UI changes.
- **Cost-Benefit Analysis:** Evaluate the costs associated with UI development against the potential benefits such as increased user engagement or revenue.
- **Risk Assessment:** Identify potential risks that could impact the UI project and develop mitigation strategies.

- **Stakeholder Alignment:** Ensure that all stakeholders are aligned on the UI business case to secure buy-in and support.
- **Implementation Plan:** Develop a detailed roadmap outlining the steps involved in implementing the UI changes.
- **Measurement and Iteration:** Plan for continuous monitoring of the UI performance and iterate based on user feedback and data analysis.
- **ROI Projection:** Estimate the return on investment (ROI) expected from the UI improvements to justify the business case.

By following these steps and presenting a comprehensive UI business case, you can increase the likelihood of successful implementation and positive outcomes for your project.

Chapter 2: User Research

2.1 User Research - 1

2.1.1. Methodologies: Qualitative and Quantitative

2.1.1.1. Qualitative Methodology:

Focuses on understanding the "why" and "how" behind a phenomenon. Involves collecting non-numerical data such as words, images, or observations. Emphasizes subjective interpretation and in-depth understanding. Uses methods like interviews, focus groups, observations, and content analysis. Results are descriptive and can provide rich insights into complex phenomena.

2.1.2. Quantitative Methodology:

- Focuses on quantifying the relationship between variables and testing hypotheses.

- Involves collecting numerical data that can be analyzed statistically. Emphasizes objectivity and generalizability of findings.
- Uses methods like surveys, experiments, and statistical analysis. Results are numerical and can be used to make predictions and generalizations about a population.

2.1.3. <u>Methodologies: Attitudes and Conduct</u>

Attitudes:

- Attitudes refer to individuals' evaluations, feelings, and tendencies towards objects or ideas.
- They can be positive, negative, or neutral and can influence behavior and decision-making.
- Attitudes are shaped by experiences, beliefs, values, and societal norms. They can be changed through education, persuasion, or personal reflection.

Conduct:

- Conduct pertains to the way individuals behave or act in various situations. It reflects one's values, ethics, and principles.
- Conduct can be influenced by attitudes, upbringing, environment, and societal expectations.
- Good conduct involves honesty, respect, fairness, and responsibility towards oneself and others.

In summary, attitudes and conduct are closely linked as attitudes can shape one's conduct and behavior. It is essential to cultivate positive attitudes and ethical conduct for personal growth, successful relationships, and societal harmony.

2.2. User Research - 2

2.2.1. User Personas

User personas are fictional representations of a target audience segment, created to understand the needs, goals, behaviors, and preferences of users. They help in designing products and services that cater to specific user groups.

Here are some key points about user personas presented simply and understandably:

- **Definition:** User personas are detailed profiles that represent different types of users who might interact with a product or service.
- **Purpose:** They help in humanizing users, understanding their motivations, and making informed design decisions.

- **Characteristics:** Personas include demographic information, behaviors, goals, pain points, and preferences of the target users.
- **Creation:** User personas are developed based on research, interviews, surveys, and data analysis to ensure accuracy.
- **Benefits:** They guide product development, marketing strategies, and communication efforts to meet user needs effectively.
- **Usage:** Personas are used by designers, marketers, and product developers to create user-centered solutions and improve user experience.

2.2.2. User Journey Mapping & Empathy Maps

User Journey Mapping:

User journey mapping is a visualization technique used to illustrate the steps and experiences a user goes through when interacting with a product or service. It helps businesses understand the user's perspective, identify pain points, and improve the overall user experience.

The process typically involves creating a timeline of touchpoints from initial awareness to post-purchase support, mapping out emotions, actions, and interactions at each stage.
User journey maps can be created using tools like diagrams, flowcharts, or digital software, and are often collaborative efforts involving stakeholders from different departments.

Empathy Maps:

Empathy maps are tools used to understand users' thoughts, feelings, and motivations by creating a visual representation of their perspective. They typically consist of four quadrants representing what the user says, thinks, does, and feels, helping businesses gain insights into the user's mindset.

Empathy maps can be created through research, interviews, or observations to gather data on user behaviors and preferences.

By using empathy maps, businesses can develop products and services that resonate with users on a deeper level, leading to more meaningful and impactful user experiences.

2.2.3. <u>User Stories & Storyboards User Stories:</u>

User stories are short, simple descriptions of a feature told from the perspective of the person who desires the new capability, usually a user or customer of the system.

They are commonly used in Agile software development to capture a description of a software feature from an end-user perspective.

User stories typically follow a simple template:

Storyboards:

Storyboards are a series of illustrations or images displayed in sequence for the purpose of pre-visualizing a motion picture, animation, or interactive media sequence.

In the context of software development and user experience design, storyboards are used to visually represent user interactions with a system.

Storyboards help communicate how a user will interact with a system, showing the flow of actions and the interface elements involved in achieving a particular task or goal.

In summary, user stories are concise descriptions of software features from a user's perspective, while storyboards are visual representations of user interactions with a system. Both tools are valuable in understanding user needs and designing user friendly software interfaces in an Agile development environment.

Chapter 3: Design and Engineering of User Experience

This chapter dives into the world of User Experience (UX) Design, a crucial aspect of creating user-friendly and intuitive digital products.

3.1. UNDERSTANDING USER EXPERIENCE DESIGN (UX DESIGN):

3.1.1 What is UX Design?

UX Design focuses on creating products that meet users' needs and preferences through user research and feedback. It's a user-centered approach to design.

3.1.2. Key aspects of UX Design:

- **User-Centered Design:** UX Design Foundation focuses on designing products that meet users' needs and preferences through user research and feedback.

- **Information Architecture:** It involves organizing and structuring content in a way that is easy to navigate and understand for users.

- **Understanding Users**: The first step in UX Design is to understand the target users of the product. This involves researching to identify their needs, behaviors, and preferences.

- **Wireframing and Prototyping**: Once the user requirements are clear, designers create wireframes and prototypes to visualize the layout and functionality of the product. This helps in testing ideas and gathering feedback early in the design process.

- **Interaction Design:** Designing interactive elements for a seamless experience.

- **Mobile Responsiveness:** Designing products that are optimized for various devices and screen sizes to provide a consistent user experience.

- **Usability Testing**: Usability testing involves observing real users interacting with the product to identify any issues or areas for improvement. This feedback is crucial for refining the design and ensuring a positive user experience.

- **Visual Design**: In this stage, designers focus on the aesthetics of the product, including colors, typography, and imagery. A visually appealing design can enhance the overall user experience and create a cohesive look and feel.

- **Accessibility and Inclusivity**: Designers also need to ensure that the product is accessible to all users, including those with disabilities. This involves following best practices for accessibility and considering the diverse needs of the user base.

- **Iterative Design Process**: UX Design is an iterative process, where designers continuously gather feedback, make improvements, and test new ideas. This cycle helps in creating a user-centered product that meets the needs of the target audience.

3.2. BENEFITS OF EFFECTIVE UX DESIGN:

- Creates user-friendly and intuitive products.
- Enhances user satisfaction and overall experience.
- Increases product adoption and user engagement.
- Drives business success through a positive user experience.

3.3. MASTERING THE UX DESIGN FOUNDATION:

User Experience (UX) Design Foundation is essential for creating user-friendly and intuitive digital products. User Experience (UX) and User Interface (UI) design are essential for successful digital products. UX focuses on improving user satisfaction through usability and accessibility, while UI focuses on visual elements.

Creating a seamless experience involves understanding the audience, designing for accessibility, and maintaining consistency. User research, personas, user flows, wireframes, and prototypes play key roles. Collaboration among designers, developers, and stakeholders is crucial for creating visually appealing and functional products that provide a positive user experience.

This section explores key concepts that form the foundation of UX Design:

3.3.1 Conceptual Models & User Models:

- **Conceptual Models:** Represent how users think about a system, helping designers create intuitive interfaces.

- **User Models:** Represent target user characteristics and behaviors, guiding design decisions.

Conceptual Models:

- Conceptual models are representations of the way users think about a system or product.
- They help designers understand users' mental models and design interfaces that align with users' expectations.
- Conceptual models are created based on research, user feedback, and iterative design processes.
- They provide a framework for organizing information and interactions within a system.
- Designers use conceptual models to create intuitive and user-friendly interfaces.

User Models:

- User models are representations of the characteristics and behaviors of the target users.
- They include demographic information, preferences, goals, and tasks users perform.
- User models help designers empathize with users and design solutions tailored to their needs.
- Designers create user personas based on user models to humanize the design process.
- User models guide design decisions to ensure the product meets users' requirements and expectations.

3.3.2 Systems Thinking & Innovation Frameworks:

- **Systems Thinking:** Understanding the interconnectedness within a system for better problem-solving.

- **Innovation Frameworks:** Structured methodologies to foster creativity and new ideas (e.g., Design Thinking, Lean Startup).

Systems Thinking - Key Concepts:

- **Mental Models:** These are the underlying assumptions, beliefs, and values that shape how individuals perceive and interact with the world.
- **Feedback Loops:** These are mechanisms through which a system responds to inputs and influences its own behavior over time.
- **Emergence:** The idea that complex behaviors and patterns can arise from interactions among simpler components within a system.
- **Benefits of Systems Thinking:** Enhances decision-making by considering the broader impact of actions. Facilitates innovation by uncovering hidden relationships and opportunities for improvement.

Types of Innovation Frameworks:

- **Design Thinking:** Focuses on empathy, ideation, and prototyping to create human-centered solutions.

- **Lean Startup:** Emphasizes rapid experimentation, validated learning, and iterative product development.

- **Agile Methodology:** Involves adaptive planning, evolutionary development, and continuous improvement in a collaborative environment.

- **Role of Mental Models and Feedback Loops:** Mental models help individuals challenge assumptions and think creatively about problems.

- Feedback loops enable organizations to learn from past experiences, adapt to changes, and drive continuous innovation.

By incorporating Systems Thinking and leveraging Innovation Frameworks, individuals and organizations can gain a deeper understanding of complex systems, foster creativity, and drive meaningful change in today's dynamic world.

3.3.3. <u>Wireframing, Prototyping & Information Architecture:</u>

- **Wireframing:** Visual representation of a web page or app layout without design elements.
- **Prototyping:** More interactive and detailed version of a wireframe, allowing for user testing.
- **Information Architecture:** Organizing and structuring content within a website or app for easy access.

Wireframing:

- Wireframing is a visual representation of a webpage or app layout without design elements like colors and images.
- It focuses on the structure and functionality of the interface.
- Wireframes help in planning the placement of elements and the user flow before moving on to design.

Prototyping:

- Prototyping is a more interactive and detailed version of a wireframe, often with clickable elements.
- It allows designers and stakeholders to test the functionality and user experience of the product.
- Prototypes can range from low-fidelity (basic layout) to high-fidelity (closely resembling the final product).

Information Architecture:

- Information architecture is the way content is organized and structured within a website or app.

- It involves categorizing information, labeling navigation, and ensuring easy access to content.

- Good information architecture enhances user experience by making it easier for users to find what they need.

These elements work together to create user-friendly and effective digital products.

3.4. DESIGN PRINCIPLES & HEURISTICS FOR USABILITY:

These principles guide designers in creating user-friendly interfaces:

1. **Visibility:** Important elements should be easy to see and access.

2. **Feedback:** Users need clear feedback for their actions.

3. **Consistency:** Maintain a consistent look and behavior throughout the design.

4. **Hierarchy:** Organize information logically with clear distinctions between levels.

5. **Simplicity:** Keep designs simple and avoid unnecessary elements.

6. Flexibility: Designs should accommodate different user needs and preferences.

7. **Error Prevention:** Anticipate and prevent errors through clear design and instructions.

8. **Recognition over Recall:** Make information and actions visible instead of relying on memory.

9. **Aesthetic and Minimalist Design:** Focus on a clean and visually appealing design for a better user experience.

By following these design principles and heuristics, designers can create engaging, user-friendly, and interactive products that cater to users' needs effectively.

3.5. DESIGN STANDARDS & GUIDELINES:

These guidelines ensure consistency, quality, and usability in design projects:

Design Standards & Guidelines are essential principles that help ensure consistency, quality, and usability in design projects. They serve as a set of rules and recommendations to follow when creating anything from websites to print materials.

Here are some key bullet points to help you understand them better:

1. **Consistency:** Design Standards promote uniformity in design elements such as colors,

fonts, and spacing to create a cohesive look and feel.

2. **Accessibility:** Guidelines ensure that designs are inclusive and can be easily accessed and understood by all users, including those with disabilities.

3. **Usability:** Standards focus on creating intuitive and user-friendly designs that enhance the overall user experience.

4. **Brand Identity:** Guidelines help maintain brand consistency by defining how logos, colors, and other brand elements should be used.

5. **Responsiveness:** Standards often include guidelines for creating designs that are responsive and adaptable to different devices and screen sizes.

6. **Compliance:** Guidelines may also cover legal requirements such as copyright laws and

industry regulations to ensure designs are compliant.

By following Design Standards & Guidelines, designers can create visually appealing, functional, and effective designs that resonate with their target audience while maintaining a level of professionalism and quality.

3.6. USABILITY & ACCESSIBILITY STUDIES:

Usability and accessibility studies play a crucial role in ensuring that websites, applications, and products are user-friendly and inclusive for all individuals.

These studies ensure websites, applications, and products are user-friendly and inclusive:

3.6.1. Usability Studies:

- Usability studies focus on how easy and efficient it is for users to accomplish tasks within a system.

- They involve observing real users interacting with a product to identify any usability issues.
- Usability studies help designers and developers understand user behavior and preferences to improve the overall user experience.
- Methods used in usability studies include user testing, interviews, surveys, and analytics data analysis.
- The goal of usability studies is to enhance user satisfaction, efficiency, and effectiveness when using a product.

3.6.2 Accessibility Studies:

- Accessibility studies concentrate on making products usable by people with disabilities, including visual, auditory, physical, and cognitive impairments. They involve evaluating how easily individuals with disabilities can navigate and interact with a product.

- Accessibility studies aim to ensure that websites and applications comply with accessibility standards such as WCAG (Web Content Accessibility Guidelines). Methods used in accessibility studies include assistive technology testing, screen reader compatibility, and keyboard navigation assessments.
- The goal of accessibility studies is to create inclusive designs that provide equal access and opportunities for all users, regardless of their abilities.

By understanding and applying these principles, you can create user-centered digital experiences, prioritize user needs by conducting research, empathizing with users, and incorporating feedback. Focus on user-friendly design elements like clear navigation and seamless interactions to enhance the overall user experience.

Chapter 4 - UI Design Foundations

Welcome to the world of UI Design! This guidebook serves as your roadmap to understanding the essential principles and practices that create effective user interfaces (UIs). We'll explore the psychology behind user behavior, build a foundation in core design principles, and delve into practical workflows for creating UIs that are both beautiful and functional.

4.1. USER INTERFACE DESIGN

User Interface Design is a critical aspect of any digital product or service, as it focuses on creating interfaces that are user-friendly, intuitive, and visually appealing.

- **User-Centered Design:** UI design starts by understanding the needs and preferences of the target users to create interfaces that meet their expectations.

- **Visual Hierarchy:** It involves organizing elements on a screen in a way that guides users' attention and helps them navigate the interface easily.
- **Consistency:** Maintaining consistency in design elements such as colors, fonts, and layouts across the interface enhances user experience and makes it easier for users to interact with the product.
- **Accessibility:** Designing interfaces that are accessible to users with disabilities ensures inclusivity and a better user experience for all.
- **Feedback and Response:** Providing feedback to user actions and keeping them informed about system status helps in creating a more interactive and engaging interface.
- **Mobile Responsiveness:** With the increasing use of mobile devices, designing interfaces that are responsive and adapt to different screen sizes is essential for a seamless user experience.

By focusing on these key points, UI designers can create interfaces that not only look visually appealing but also ensure a smooth and engaging user experience for the target audience.

4.2. UNDERSTANDING USERS AND THEIR NEEDS

4.2.1. User-Centered Design (UCD):

Our journey begins with understanding the core philosophy of UCD. This approach places users at the center of the design process, ensuring every decision is driven by their needs and goals. We'll explore methodologies like user research (surveys, interviews, A/B testing) to gather valuable insights and translate them into actionable design solutions.

4.2.2. Information Architecture (IA):

Creating a user interface requires a well-organized foundation. IA focuses on structuring content in a logical and hierarchical manner, ensuring users can find what they need intuitively. We'll delve into techniques like sitemaps, user flows, and navigation design to create a seamless user journey.

4.2.3. Interaction Design (IxD):

Beyond visual aesthetics, UI design encompasses the user's interaction with the interface. IxD focuses on designing the behaviors and reactions of the interface, creating a delightful and intuitive experience for users. This includes elements like microinteractions, animation, and user flows.

4.3. BUILDING A STRONG UI FOUNDATION

4.3.1. Gestalt's Principles of Design:

Psychology plays a crucial role in UI design. Gestalt principles offer a set of visual design guidelines that leverage the way humans perceive information. These principles, like proximity, similarity, and closure, help us create interfaces that are visually organized and easy to understand.

- **Proximity**: Elements placed closer together are perceived as related.
- **Similarity**: Elements with similar visual characteristics are perceived as belonging together.
- **Closure**: Our brains tend to fill in gaps to perceive a complete whole.
- **Continuity**: Elements arranged along a visual path are perceived as related.
- **Figure-ground**: Users distinguish between the foreground (the element in focus) and the background.

4.3.2. Visual Design Principles

Building on the foundation of Gestalt principles, we'll explore core visual design elements that bring your UI to life.

These include:

- **Typography:** Choosing the right fonts and text styles creates a cohesive and readable interface.
- **Color Theory:** Colors evoke emotions and influence user behavior. We'll explore color psychology and learn to create effective color palettes.
- **Layout and White Space:** Effective layout utilizes white space strategically to improve visual hierarchy and guide the user's eye.
- **Imagery and Iconography:** Integrating captivating visuals enhances user engagement and reinforces branding.

4.4. DESIGN SYSTEMS FOR CONSISTENCY AND EFFICIENCY

4.4.1. What are Design Systems?

Design systems are a collection of reusable components, guidelines, and code that unify the look and feel of a product across all platforms. They promote consistency, streamline workflows, and ensure brand coherence.

4.4.2. Components and Libraries:

Design systems organize UI elements into reusable components (buttons, forms, etc.) stored in libraries for easy access and implementation across the product.

4.4.3. Style Guides:

Style guides define the visual language of your product. They include typography styles, color palettes, spacing guidelines, and logo usage rules to maintain brand consistency.

4.4.4. Building and Maintaining Design Systems:

We'll explore strategies for creating and maintaining effective design systems, fostering collaboration between designers, developers, and other stakeholders.

4.5 FROM MOCKUPS TO DEVELOPMENT: Handoff and Collaboration

4.5.1. Design Tools and Prototyping:

User Interface design relies heavily on tools like Figma, Sketch, Adobe XD for creating mockups, high-fidelity prototypes, and interactive wireframes. These tools allow designers to visualize UI concepts and gather user feedback before development begins.

4.5.2. Developer Handoff:

Once designs are finalized, it's time for the handoff to development teams. This involves creating detailed specifications, assets libraries, and style guides to ensure developers understand the intent and functionality behind each design element.

4.5.3. Communication and Collaboration:

Effective communication and collaboration are crucial between designers and developers. We'll explore strategies for clear documentation, maintaining a central source of truth for design assets, and fostering a collaborative environment.

4.6. BRANDING THROUGH UI DESIGN

4.6.1. The Power of Brand Identity:

UI design plays a vital role in communicating your brand identity. Every visual element, from typography to color palette to layout, contributes to the overall user experience and brand perception.

Chapter 5 - Design Testing and Evaluation:

Effective design doesn't happen in a vacuum. Testing and evaluation are crucial steps in the design process, ensuring your creations meet user needs and achieve the desired outcomes. This chapter explores various design testing and evaluation methods, helping you refine your designs and deliver exceptional user experiences.

5.1 THE IMPORTANCE OF DESIGN TESTING AND EVALUATION

Why test and evaluate designs? Here are some compelling reasons:

- **Identify Usability Issues:** Early testing helps uncover usability problems before significant development investment. This saves time, resources, and rework later in the process.

- **Validate Design Decisions:** Testing allows you to gather data on user behavior and validate your design assumptions. This data helps confirm if your design choices are effective.

- **Improve User Experience:** Testing provides valuable insights into user needs and preferences. By iterating based on test results, you can create a more user-friendly and enjoyable experience.

- **Increase Design Confidence:** Testing provides evidence to support your design decisions. This data empowers you to present your designs with greater confidence to stakeholders.

- **Reduce Development Costs:** Identifying and fixing usability issues early reduces the need for costly redesigns later in the development lifecycle.

5.2 TYPES OF DESIGN TESTING AND EVALUATION

There are various approaches to design testing and evaluation, each with its strengths and weaknesses. Selecting the most appropriate method depends on the project stage, resources available, and specific goals. Here's an overview of common techniques:

5.2.1 Usability Testing

Usability testing involves observing real users interact with your design prototype or live product. The goal is to assess how easy and intuitive it is for users to achieve their desired tasks.

- **Methods:** Individual user testing, group usability testing, remote usability testing tools.
- **Benefits:** Provides rich qualitative data on user behavior and thinking processes.

- **Limitations:** Can be time-consuming and expensive depending on the number of users tested.

5.2.2 Heuristic Evaluation

Heuristic evaluation involves usability experts reviewing your design against established design principles (heuristics) to identify potential usability problems.

- **Methods:** Experts conduct individual reviews or collaborate in a group setting.
- **Benefits:** Efficient and cost-effective way to identify major usability issues early in the design process.
- **Limitations:** Relies on the expertise of the evaluators and may miss user-specific issues.

5.2.3 A/B Testing

A/B testing involves presenting two or more variations of a design element (e.g., button layout, call to action message) to a portion of your user base and collecting data on which version performs better.

- **Methods:** Implement variations of the design element on your website or app and track user behavior metrics (clicks, conversions) through analytics tools.
- **Benefits:** Provides quantitative data on user behavior and helps determine the most effective design variant.
- **Limitations:** Requires a large user base for statistically significant results and may not be suitable for complex design decisions.

5.2.4 User Surveys and Interviews

User surveys and interviews aim to gather feedback from users regarding their perception of the design. Surveys usually focus on quantitative data, gathering information on user satisfaction or preferences through questionnaires. On the other hand, interviews are qualitative, enabling users to articulate their thoughts and emotions in an open-ended manner.

- **Methods:** Online surveys, in-person interviews, phone interviews.
- **Benefits:** Provides insights into user attitudes, expectations, and pain points.
- **Limitations:** Surveys can be susceptible to biases, and interviews require careful design to gather reliable information.

5.3 PLANNING AND CONDUCTING EFFECTIVE DESIGN TESTING

To maximize the effectiveness of your design testing, consider these key steps:

- **Define Testing Goals:** Clearly identify what you want to learn from the testing session. Are you focusing on specific user flows, information architecture, or overall user experience?
- **Recruit Participants:** Select participants that represent your target user base. Consider factors like demographics, technical skills, and experience level.
- **Develop Test Scenarios:** Create a set of tasks or scenarios that users will complete during the testing session. These tasks should reflect typical user goals and interactions.
- **Prepare Testing Materials:** Prepare prototypes, mockups, or live product versions for testing.

Additionally, have any necessary testing scripts or instructions ready.

- **Conduct the Test Session:** Moderate the testing session, guiding users through the tasks while observing their behavior and capturing feedback.

- **Analyze and Interpret Results:** Once testing is complete, analyze the data collected (observations, recordings, user feedback). Identify recurring patterns and usability issues that require addressing.

5.4 TOOLS AND RESOURCES FOR DESIGN TESTING AND EVALUATION

- **Usability Testing Platforms:** UserTesting, Lookback, Maze (provide tools for remote usability testing with user recruitment and data analysis features).

- **Analytics Tools:** Google Analytics, Hotjar (track user behavior on websites and apps, providing insights into user interactions and click-through rates).

- **Survey Tools:** SurveyMonkey, Typeform (create and distribute online surveys to gather user feedback on design concepts or prototypes).

- **Heatmaps and Session Recordings:** Hotjar, Crazy Egg (visualize user behavior by capturing heatmaps of user clicks and recordings of user sessions).

- **Accessibility Testing Tools:** WAVE, aXe (identify accessibility issues in your designs to ensure they are usable by users with disabilities).

5.5 THE ITERATIVE DESIGN PROCESS

Design testing and evaluation are not isolated occurrences; instead, they form part of an iterative process within the broader design workflow. Here's how they integrate into the larger scheme:

1. **Ideation and Research:** Through user research and brainstorming, you generate design ideas and initial concepts.
2. **Prototyping:** Create low-fidelity or high-fidelity prototypes to represent your design concepts.
3. **Testing and Evaluation:** Conduct user testing and evaluation on your prototypes to gather feedback and identify areas for improvement.
4. **Iteration:** Based on test results, refine and iterate on your designs, addressing identified issues and incorporating user feedback.
5. **Implementation:** Once designs are finalized, develop and launch the final product or website.

5.6 CONCLUSION

By actively integrating design testing and evaluation into your process, you gain valuable insights into user behavior and preferences. This allows you to create user-centered designs that are not only aesthetically pleasing but also functional, intuitive, and ultimately successful in achieving your design goals.

Bonus Section: Advanced Design Testing Techniques

For those interested in delving deeper, here's a brief overview of some advanced design testing techniques:

- **Card Sorting:** Helps understand how users categorize information and organize content.
- **Eye-Tracking:** Reveals where users focus their attention on your design, identifying areas of interest and potential confusion points.
- **Tree Testing:** Evaluates the information architecture of your website or app by testing users' ability to navigate and find specific content.

Remember: The selection of a testing method relies on the particular requirements and resources of your project. By integrating different testing and evaluation methods during the design phase, you can guarantee that your designs are not only visually appealing but also user-friendly and effective in fulfilling their intended goals.

Chapter 6: Digital Product Management: A Guide for UX Designers

In today's digital world, the success of any product relies on a strong partnership between UX Designers and Product Managers. While these roles have distinct duties, grasping the fundamental principles of digital product management enables UX Designers to contribute effectively and deliver outstanding user experiences. This segment delves into the realm of digital product management, equipping UX Designers with the essential knowledge to become valuable collaborators in the product development journey.

6.1 Understanding Digital Product Management

- Digital product management involves strategic planning, development, launch, and continuous optimization of digital products like websites, mobile apps, and software applications.

- Product Managers serve as the link between different stakeholders:

  - **Users:** Understanding user needs and ensuring value delivery.

  - **Business Goals:** Aligning product development with business objectives and market opportunities.

  - **Development Team:** Communicating product vision and requirements to developers, engineers, and designers.

6.2 Key Responsibilities of a Digital Product Manager

- Product Managers juggle multiple responsibilities, including:

- **Market and User Research:** Identifying user needs, opportunities, and the competitive landscape.

- **Product Strategy and Vision:** Defining product vision, roadmap, and long-term goals.

- **Prioritization and Backlog Management:** Ranking features based on user needs, business impact, and feasibility.

- **UX Design Collaboration:** Working closely with UX Designers to align product design with user needs and business objectives.

- **Development and Iteration:** Collaborating with development teams to implement product designs.

- **Product Launch and Growth:** Overseeing the launch, monitoring user data, and iterating based on feedback.

6.3 Integration of UX Design in Digital Product Management

- UX Designers play a vital role throughout the product development process, collaborating with Product Managers at every phase:
  - **Early Planning:** Collaborating on user needs, competitor analysis, and market research to shape initial design directions.
  - **Information Architecture:** Defining user flows for a seamless experience.
  - **Prototyping and Testing:** Creating prototypes, conducting user tests, and refining designs based on feedback.
  - **Design Handoff:** Providing developers with design specifications for implementation.
  - **Post-Launch Analysis:** Analyzing user data post-launch for UX improvements.

6.4 Advantages of UX Designers Understanding Digital Product Management

- Understanding product management benefits UX Designers in various ways:
  - **Effective Communication:** Shared terminology and understanding enhance communication with Product Managers.
  - **Informed Decisions:** Consideration of business goals and technical feasibility leads to better design decisions.
  - **Problem Solving:** Anticipating challenges and collaborating on solutions.
  - **Value Demonstration:** Showcasing the impact of UX design on user experience and product success.
  - **Career Growth:** Broader understanding enhances career prospects.

6.5 Collaboration Tips for UX Designers and Product Managers

- Effective collaboration tips include:
  - **Communication:** Establish open channels and share information proactively.
  - **Shared Goals:** Align on the product vision and objectives.
  - **Respect Expertise:** Value each other's expertise and contributions.
  - **User Research:** Collaborate on research activities to understand user needs.
  - **Embrace Iteration:** Adapt designs based on feedback and evolving requirements.

Bonus Section: Essential Tools for Digital Product Managers

- **User Research Tools:** UserTesting, Lookback (facilitate remote user testing and gather user feedback).
- **Analytics Tools:** Google Analytics, Mixpanel (track user behavior on websites and apps, providing insights into user engagement and product performance).
- **Prototyping Tools:** Figma, Adobe XD, InVision (enable creating interactive prototypes to test and refine user flows).
- **Communication Tools:** Slack, Microsoft Teams (facilitate real-time communication and collaboration within teams).

6.7 The Future of UX Design and Digital Product Management

The digital landscape is constantly evolving, and both UX Design and Digital Product Management are dynamic fields. Here are some trends to keep an eye on:

- **Focus on User Experience (UX) Everywhere:** User experience will continue to be a top priority across all touchpoints, from websites and apps to voice interfaces and wearable technology.
- **Data-Driven Design Decisions:** Data analytics will play an increasingly crucial role in informing design decisions and measuring the effectiveness of UX design interventions.
- **Design Thinking Integration:** The principles of design thinking will be further integrated into product development processes, fostering collaboration and user-centric innovation.
- **Rise of Agile Methodologies:** Agile development methodologies will continue to dominate, requiring UX Designers and Product Managers to work in an iterative and adaptable manner.

- **The Expanding Role of UX Design:** UX Designers will likely take on broader roles, potentially including user research specialization, design systems management, and even product strategy contribution.

By staying informed about these trends and continuously developing their skillsets, UX Designers can position themselves as strategic partners within the digital product development ecosystem.

Conclusion

In conclusion, understanding the principles of digital product management empowers UX Designers to become more valuable contributors to the product development process. Through effective collaboration and communication with Product Managers, UX Designers can play a pivotal role in crafting exceptional user experiences that drive product success and shape the future of digital products.

Chapter 7: Designing for Next-Gen Technologies

The technological landscape is constantly evolving, presenting exciting opportunities for UX Designers. This chapter explores the world of next-gen technologies and how UX Design principles can be applied to create intuitive and user-friendly experiences for these emerging platforms.

7.1 Understanding Next-Gen Technologies

Next-gen technologies encompass a diverse range of innovations that are poised to redefine how we interact with the digital world. Here are some key areas shaping the future of user experience design:

- **Artificial Intelligence (AI):** AI encompasses various subfields like machine learning, natural language processing, and computer vision. AI-powered interfaces are transforming user experiences through features like chatbots, intelligent assistants, and personalized recommendations.

- **Virtual Reality (VR) and Augmented Reality (AR):** VR immerses users in a completely simulated environment, while AR overlays digital elements onto the real world. Both technologies offer exciting possibilities for gaming, education, training, and product visualization.

- **The Internet of Things (IoT):** The IoT connects everyday devices to the internet, enabling them to collect and share data. UX Designers need to consider how users will interact with and manage these interconnected devices.

- **Voice User Interfaces (VUIs):** VUIs allow users to interact with technology using voice commands. This technology is becoming increasingly popular with smart speakers, virtual assistants, and voice-controlled interfaces in various devices.

- **Wearable Technology:** Smartwatches, fitness trackers, and other wearable devices are becoming increasingly popular. UX Designers need to consider the unique interaction methods and design constraints of these wearable devices.

7.2 Design Considerations for Next-Gen Technologies

Designing for next-gen technologies requires careful consideration of various factors:

- **User Needs and Expectations:** Understanding user needs and mental models for interacting with new technologies is crucial for creating intuitive experiences.
- **Natural User Interfaces (NUIs):** Designing interfaces that mimic natural human interactions (touch, voice, gesture) is key for seamless user experiences.
- **Accessibility and Inclusivity:** Ensure next-gen experiences are accessible to users with disabilities, considering diverse physical abilities and sensory needs.

- **Data Privacy and Security:** As technology collects more user data, designing interfaces with clear data privacy practices and robust security measures is paramount.
- **Content Design and Storytelling:** Craft compelling narratives and tailor content formats (visual, auditory) to suit the specific next-gen platform.

7.3 Designing for Specific Next-Gen Technologies

Here's a deeper dive into applying UX design principles to some key next-gen technologies:

- **Designing for AI:** Focus on transparency and explainability of AI-powered features. Users should understand how AI works and feel comfortable interacting with it.
- **Designing for VR/AR:** Prioritize visual comfort, create intuitive ways to navigate virtual environments, and consider potential physical side effects of extended use.

- **Designing for IoT:** Design user interfaces that are easy to understand and navigate on a variety of devices. Consider data visualization and user control over connected devices.
- **Designing for VUIs:** Focus on natural language understanding, clear error correction mechanisms, and user feedback on voice commands.
- **Designing for Wearables:** Prioritize limited screen space, optimize for touch or voice interaction, and consider energy efficiency for battery-powered devices.

7.4 The Role of Prototyping and User Testing in Next-Gen Design

Prototyping plays a vital role in exploring user interaction with next-gen technologies. Here are some specific considerations:

- **Rapid Prototyping:** Utilize low-fidelity prototypes to quickly test core interaction concepts and user flows for next-gen interfaces.

- **Simulations and Emulations:** Leverage VR/AR development tools to create simulations or emulations to test user experiences within these immersive environments.

- **User Testing with Specialized Equipment:** User testing for VR/AR or wearables may require specialized equipment and controlled environments to provide realistic testing scenarios.

7.5 The Future of UX Design and Next-Gen Technologies

As technology evolves, so too will the role of UX Designers. Here's what the future holds:

- **UX Design Specialization:** UX Designers may specialize in specific next-gen technologies, developing deep expertise in user experience design for VR/AR, AI, or wearable devices.

- **UX Design for Emerging Platforms:** UX Designers will need to be adaptable and open to learning new design paradigms as novel technologies emerge.

- **The Human Touch in a Tech-Driven World:** Despite technological advancements, the human element in design remains crucial. UX Designers will continue to champion user needs and ensure ethical and human-centered design principles guide interactions with next-gen technology.

7.6 Conclusion

By understanding these technologies, their design constraints, and user needs, UX Designers can play a critical role in shaping the future of human-computer interaction. Through continuous learning, experimentation, and a focus on user-centered design principles, UX Designers can ensure that next-gen technologies are not just technologically advanced but also intuitive, accessible, and truly user-friendly.

Bonus Section: Resources for Learning About Next-Gen Technologies

Staying informed about the latest advancements in next-gen technologies is crucial for UX Designers. Here are some helpful resources:

- **Industry Publications and Blogs:** Follow publications and blogs focused on emerging technologies, such as Wired, MIT Technology Review, and UX Collective.

- **Online Courses and Workshops:** Enroll in online courses or workshops offered by platforms like Coursera, Udacity, and Interaction Design Foundation to gain deeper knowledge about specific next-gen technologies like VR/AR or AI design.

- **Conferences and Events:** Attend industry conferences and events focused on user experience and emerging technologies to connect with other professionals and learn from leading experts.

- **Virtual Reality (VR) and Augmented Reality (AR) Development Tools:** Familiarize yourself with VR/AR development platforms like Unity, Unreal Engine, and ARKit to understand the capabilities and limitations of these technologies.

Remember: The field of next-gen technology is constantly evolving. By staying curious, embracing lifelong learning, and actively seeking out new knowledge, UX Designers can position themselves at the forefront of shaping the future of user experiences.

Chapter 8: Design Leadership

Welcome, design trailblazers! This chapter equips you with the knowledge and tools to become exceptional design leaders. You'll embark on a journey to develop the core competencies needed to foster a thriving design team, leverage design thinking for strategic advantage, and master communication skills to influence key stakeholders.

8.1: The Pillars of Design Leadership

8.1.1. From Designer to Design Leader: The Mindset Shift

The transition from individual contributor to design leader requires a significant shift in mindset. While excelling in design execution remains valuable, design leaders take a broader perspective, focusing on:

- **Strategic Vision:** Guiding the design team's direction to seamlessly align with the overall business strategy. This involves translating business goals into design objectives that drive user-centric solutions.

- **Team Management:** Creating a supportive and inspiring environment that empowers designers to excel. This includes fostering collaboration, open communication, and professional growth opportunities.

- **Mentorship and Coaching:** Nurturing the talent within your team by providing guidance, constructive feedback, and fostering a culture of continuous learning. Effective coaching empowers designers to reach their full potential and tackle complex challenges.

- **Communication and Influence:** Clearly communicating design decisions and effectively advocating for design within the organization. Design leaders act as bridges between the design team and other departments, ensuring design thinking is valued and integrated throughout the development process.

8.1.2. Building and Empowering Design Teams

A strong design team is the foundation upon which design leadership success is built. Here, you'll delve into strategies for:

- **Team Structure and Culture:** Building a diverse and inclusive design team fosters a wider range of perspectives and sparks innovation. Cultivate a collaborative and supportive environment where designers feel comfortable sharing ideas and taking risks.

- **Talent Acquisition and Retention:** Recruit top design talent by showcasing your company culture, design vision, and opportunities for professional growth. Once you've assembled a stellar team, prioritize retention strategies to keep them engaged and motivated. This may involve offering competitive compensation packages, providing opportunities for skill development, and fostering a sense of purpose within the team.

- **Performance Management and Feedback:** Providing clear performance expectations and offering constructive feedback empowers designers to understand their strengths and areas for improvement. Regularly scheduled performance reviews coupled with ongoing coaching conversations are crucial for individual growth and team development.

8.2: Design Thinking for Strategic Advantage

8.2.1. Design Thinking as a Leadership Framework

Design thinking is a human-centered approach to problem-solving that emphasizes empathy, creativity, and iterative prototyping. Learn how to leverage design thinking as a leadership framework to:

- **Identify Strategic Opportunities:** Utilize design research methods like user interviews, surveys, and usability testing to understand user needs and identify unmet opportunities. This user empathy translates into business opportunities that position your organization for success.

- **Drive Innovation:** Foster a culture of experimentation and iteration within your team. Encourage brainstorming sessions, rapid prototyping, and user testing to generate creative solutions to complex challenges. By embracing a "fail-fast, learn-fast" mentality, your team can arrive at innovative solutions that truly address user needs.

- **Communicate the Value of Design:** Articulate a compelling narrative that showcases how design thinking can drive business growth and achieve a competitive advantage. Demonstrate the positive impact of design on key metrics (e.g., user engagement, conversion rates, customer satisfaction) to gain buy-in from stakeholders.

8.2.2. Integrating Design Thinking into the Organization

The power of design thinking extends beyond the design team. Here, you'll discover strategies for integrating this approach across the organization:

- **Collaboration with Cross-Functional Teams:** Break down silos and encourage collaboration with teams like product, marketing, and engineering. By integrating design thinking into the entire product development process, you ensure user-centered considerations are prioritized at every stage.

- **Building Design Literacy:** Educate and empower other departments to understand the value of design thinking and user-centered approaches. Workshops, training sessions, and knowledge-sharing initiatives can help bridge the gap between design and other disciplines.

8.3: Mastering the Art of Communication

8.3.1. Communicating Design with Confidence

Effective communication is a cornerstone of design leadership. Master the art of presenting your design ideas with clarity, persuasion, and passion:

- **Storytelling for Design Impact:** Tell compelling stories that showcase the user journey, the problem being addressed, and the design solution's value proposition. Utilize storytelling techniques to connect with your audience on an emotional level and gain buy-in for your design vision.

- **Tailoring Communication to Your Audience:** Adapt your communication style and level of detail to resonate with different stakeholders. Executives may require a high-level overview, while engineers might benefit from a more technical explanation. Understanding your audience'

- **Visual Communication Skills:** Utilize effective visuals (mockups, prototypes, data visualizations) to enhance your design presentations. Compelling visuals can significantly improve audience understanding and retention of your message.

8.3.2. Managing Stakeholders and Advocacy

Design leaders navigate relationships with various stakeholders, each with their own interests and priorities. Here, you'll learn strategies for:

- **Stakeholder Management:** Building strong relationships with key stakeholders (executives, product managers, marketing teams) is crucial. Proactively understand their needs and priorities, manage expectations, and keep them informed about the design process.

- **Negotiation and Influence:** Design leaders often need to negotiate for design resources, budget, and timelines. Develop strong negotiation and influence skills to ensure design considerations are prioritized within the decision-making process. Frame your arguments around data, user research findings, and the potential return on investment (ROI) of design-focused solutions.

- **Building Executive Sponsorship:** Cultivating strong relationships with executives who champion the value of design within the organization is vital. Regularly communicate design's impact on business goals and secure their support for design initiatives. Executive sponsors can be powerful advocates for design thinking and user-centered approaches throughout the organization.

Conclusion

Design leadership is an exciting journey filled with opportunities to make a significant impact. By honing your leadership skills, fostering a thriving team environment, and championing the power of design thinking, you can become a catalyst for innovation and guide your organization towards a future built on human-centered design principles. Remember, continuous learning and adaptation are key to success in this ever-evolving field. Embrace the challenge and inspire your team to create groundbreaking designs that not only transform the world but also improve the lives of the users you serve.

Chapter 9: Deep Dive into Design Principles

This chapter delves into the core concepts that shape successful user experiences: the design process and fundamental design principles for User Interface (UI) and User Experience (UX) design.

9.1. The Design Process: A User-Centered Approach

The design process is a systematic framework for creating new projects. It typically follows five key stages:

1. **Empathize:** This stage focuses on understanding the users' needs, thoughts, and feelings. Designers conduct user research through interviews, surveys, and observations to gain insights into user experiences and pain points.

2. **Define:** Based on the gathered information, designers define the core problem to be addressed. This stage involves synthesizing research data into a clear and concise problem statement that guides the design direction.

3. **Ideate:** Here, designers generate a wide range of creative solutions to tackle the defined problem. Brainstorming sessions, sketching, and other techniques are used to explore various possibilities.

4. **Prototype:** Rough drafts or models (prototypes) are created to visualize how potential solutions might function in practice. Prototypes can range from low-fidelity sketches and wireframes to more advanced interactive models, depending on project complexity.

5. **Test:** Finally, prototypes are tested with real users to gather feedback and identify areas for improvement. User testing helps refine designs

through iterative cycles, ensuring the final product effectively addresses user needs.

By following these user-centered design principles, designers can create innovative and user-friendly solutions that resonate with their target audience.

9.2. Design Principles: The Building Blocks of User Experience

Design principles are fundamental guidelines that contribute to user-friendly and visually appealing digital experiences. Here's a breakdown of key UI and UX design principles:

UI Design Principles:

1. **User-Centered Design:** This principle emphasizes prioritizing the needs and preferences of users throughout the design process. Understanding user goals, motivations, and behaviors is crucial for creating a seamless and intuitive experience.

2. **Simplicity:** Clean and minimalistic interfaces with minimal clutter enhance user focus on essential elements. Prioritize clarity and avoid overwhelming users with excessive information or complex design elements.

3. **Consistency:** Maintaining consistency in design elements like colors, fonts, and layouts across the interface fosters user familiarity and intuitive navigation.

4. **Hierarchy:** Utilize visual cues like size, color, and placement to establish a clear hierarchy of elements, guiding users through the interface and emphasizing important information.

5. **Accessibility:** Design for inclusivity by considering color contrast, font size, and keyboard navigation. This ensures all users, including those with disabilities, can easily interact with the interface.

6. **Usability:** Prioritize conducting user testing and incorporating feedback to design an intuitive and efficient interface with the end user in mind.

7. **Feedback and Iteration:** Gather user feedback and analytics data to continuously iterate and improve design for an enhanced user experience. Utilize animations, sounds, or visual cues to provide instant feedback on user actions.

8. **Performance:** Fast loading times and smooth interactions are crucial for optimal design performance. Optimize code, compress media files, and leverage browser caching for a seamless user experience.

UX Design Principles:

User-Centered Design :

- Conduct user research (surveys, interviews, usability testing) to understand user behavior and expectations.

- Create user personas representing target audience segments and tailor designs to their specific needs.
- Continuously gather feedback and iterate on designs based on user preferences and evolving needs.
- Prioritize usability and accessibility for a seamless experience for all users, regardless of ability.

Additional UX Design Considerations:

- **Simplicity:** A clean and uncluttered interface minimizes cognitive load and improves user comprehension.
- **Consistency:** Maintaining consistency in design language across the platform reinforces user familiarity and intuitive navigation.
- **Hierarchy:** Establishing a clear hierarchy of elements using size, color, and placement

ensures users understand the relative importance of information.

- **Accessibility:** Incorporate accessibility features like high color contrast, adjustable font sizes, keyboard navigation, and alternative text for images to create an inclusive interface.
- **Usability:** Conduct user testing and prioritize user feedback to optimize the user experience for efficient task completion.
- **Feedback and Iteration:** Utilize user testing, analytics, and feedback mechanisms to continuously refine the design and address user pain points.

By understanding and applying these design principles, you can create user interfaces that are not only visually appealing but also intuitive, efficient, and accessible, ultimately resulting in a positive user experience.

Chapter 10 - Designing a Low Fidelity Prototype in Figma

Create a low-fidelity prototype in Figma by following specific tasks in the project.

1. Create an account in Figma
2. UI element drawing on a mobile device
3. Adding elements in your design
4. UI designs made with UI kits
5. Creating a user interface with basic components and parts
6. Showcasing your prototypes to interested parties
7. Transferring your completed prototype
8. Creating an A/B test user interface

1: Create an account in Figma

Step 1: Go to the Figma website at www.figma.com
Step 2: Click on the "Sign Up" button located at the top right corner of the page
Step 3: Enter your email address, create a password, and click on "Sign Up"

Step 4: Check your email inbox for a verification email from Figma

Step 5: Click on the verification link in the email to activate your Figma account

Step 6: Once your account is activated, you can start using Figma to create stunning designs and collaborate with others

Step 7: Explore the various features and tools available in Figma to unleash your creativity and design skills

Congratulations! You have successfully created an account in Figma and are now ready to dive into the world of digital design.

2: UI element drawing on a mobile device

Before adding user interface (UI) elements to your mobile screen, it is crucial to understand the basic principles of UI design. Start by sketching out the layout of your mobile screen on paper to organize components such as buttons, text fields, and images strategically. Pay attention to visual hierarchy to highlight important elements for improved user accessibility.

Leverage design software such as Adobe XD, Sketch, or Figma to craft digital prototypes of your UI design before its implementation on the mobile screen. Delve into details like color palettes, typography, spacing, and uniformity to craft an aesthetically pleasing and intuitive interface.

Verify the compatibility and responsiveness of your UI design across diverse mobile devices by conducting thorough testing.

Refine your design iteratively based on user feedback and usability assessments to enhance the user experience and implement necessary enhancements for a polished final rendition.

3. Adding Elements in Your Design

Adding elements to your UI design is a crucial step in creating a functional and visually appealing interface. Here's a breakdown of the process:

- **Planning and Prioritization:** Start by identifying the core functionalities and content your UI needs to present. Prioritize elements based on their importance to user tasks and the overall information hierarchy.

- **Choosing the Right Elements:** Select UI elements that best suit the purpose and user interaction for each section. Common UI elements include buttons, text fields, menus, icons, images, and progress bars.

- **Positioning and Layout:** Arrange elements strategically on the screen considering user flow, visual hierarchy, and aesthetics. Utilize white space effectively to prevent clutter and guide users' attention.

- **Applying Styles:** Apply consistent styles (colors, fonts, sizes) to your elements according to your design system or brand guidelines. This ensures visual harmony and reinforces user recognition.

- **Maintaining Consistency:** Maintain consistency in element size, spacing, and behavior across the entire UI. This fosters user familiarity and intuitive navigation.

- **Testing and Iteration:** Continuously test your design with users to identify any usability issues with element placement or interaction. Be prepared to iterate and refine the layout based on feedback.

4. UI Designs Made with UI Kits

UI Kits are pre-made collections of UI elements designed for a specific platform (e.g., iOS, Android) or style (e.g., flat design, neumorphism). They offer designers a jumpstart by providing a set of ready-to-use components that can be customized for their projects.

Benefits of Using UI Kits:

- **Efficiency:** UI Kits save designers time by offering pre-built elements instead of creating them from scratch.
- **Consistency:** Kits ensure consistent design language with standardized styles and components.
- **Quality:** Many UI Kits are professionally designed and offer high-quality assets.

Things to Consider When Using UI Kits:

- **Customization:** While offering a base, UI Kits should be customizable to fit your specific design needs and brand identity.
- **Originality:** Avoid using generic kits that might make your design look unoriginal.
- **License:** Always check the license agreement before using a UI Kit to ensure proper usage rights.

5. Creating a User Interface with Basic Components and Parts

Even without complex design tools, you can build functional UIs using basic components. Here's what you'll typically need:

- **Containers:** Containers group related elements and create a visual hierarchy. Common containers include boxes, cards, and panels.
- **Text Elements:** Text is a core component for displaying information and labels. Use clear typefaces and appropriate sizes for readability.
- **Buttons:** Buttons allow users to initiate actions. Design clear and visually distinct buttons for different functionalities.
- **Input Fields:** Input fields enable users to enter data. Design them based on the type of data expected (text, numbers, dates, etc.).

- **Images and Icons:** Use visuals strategically to enhance user experience and break up text content. Ensure icons are clear and understandable.

By combining these basic components effectively, you can create surprisingly functional and user-friendly UIs.

6. Showcasing Your Prototypes to Interested Parties

Prototypes are crucial for communicating your design vision to stakeholders and gathering feedback. Here are some tips for showcasing them:

- **Prepare a Contextual Presentation:** Provide a brief introduction explaining the project goals and target audience.
- **Choose the Right Platform:** Select a prototyping tool (online tools, interactive mockups) that best

suits the complexity of your prototype and the audience's technical expertise.

- **Focus on User Flow:** Guide viewers through the prototype, demonstrating key user actions and functionalities.

- **Encourage Feedback:** Actively encourage questions and feedback from stakeholders. This helps identify areas for improvement before final development.

- **Be Prepared to Address Concerns:** Anticipate potential questions and have explanations ready for design decisions.

7. Transferring Your Completed Prototype

Once your prototype is finalized, you might need to transfer it to developers for implementation. Here are some options:

- **Design Handoff Tools:** Utilize design handoff tools that allow exporting specifications (styles, assets, measurements) for developers.
- **Detailed Documentation:** Create comprehensive documentation outlining design decisions, user flows, and interactions.
- **Live Prototyping Tools:** If your prototyping tool allows live previews or code generation, it can directly facilitate development.

8. Creating an A/B Test User Interface

A/B testing involves presenting two variations of a UI to different user groups (to A/B testing UI): to measure which version performs better based on a predefined goal (e.g., increased conversions, improved user engagement). Here's a breakdown of creating a UI specifically for A/B testing:

Planning the A/B Test UI:

1. **Define the Hypothesis:** Clearly define what aspect of the UI you want to test. It could be a button design, layout change, or the wording of a call to action.

2. **Identify the Metric:** Determine the metric you'll use to measure success. This could be click-through rate, conversion rate, time spent on a page, or any relevant user action.

3. **Design the Variations:** Create two (or more) variations of the UI element you're testing. Ensure the variations are visually distinct but maintain overall design consistency.

Building the A/B Test UI:

1. **Utilize A/B Testing Tools:** Leverage A/B testing tools that allow you to create variations and randomly assign them to user groups. These tools also track user interaction data for analysis.

2. **Develop Responsive Variations:** Ensure your UI variations are responsive and adapt seamlessly to different screen sizes and devices used by your target audience.

3. **Maintain Brand Consistency:** While testing variations, maintain the overall brand identity and design language to avoid confusing users.

Running the A/B Test:

1. **Set a Sample Size:** Determine a statistically significant sample size for the test to ensure reliable results.

2. **Monitor Performance:** Closely monitor the A/B test throughout its duration, tracking user interactions and the chosen success metric.

3. **Analyze the Results:** Once sufficient data is collected, analyze the results to determine which UI variation performed better based on your chosen metric.

Following the A/B Test:

1. **Implement the Winner:** Integrate the UI variation that yielded the best results into your main product or service.

2. **Consider Further Testing:** A/B testing is an iterative process. You can use the learnings from this test to refine your UI further and conduct additional tests with new hypotheses.

3. **Document the Findings:** Document the A/B testing process, results, and learnings for future reference and to inform future design decisions.

By following these steps, you can create effective A/B test UIs and leverage data-driven insights to optimize your user interface for better performance and user experience.

Acknowledgement

Writing a book is a team effort, and I would like to take this opportunity to express my gratitude to everyone who helped make this project possible.

First and foremost, I would like to thank my family and friends for their unwavering support throughout the writing process. Their encouragement and understanding helped me stay motivated and focused on the task at hand.

I am grateful to the team at the publisher for their guidance and support throughout the publishing process. Their dedication to producing high-quality educational materials is truly admirable.

Last but not least, I would like to thank the readers of this book. I hope that the knowledge and skills you gain from these pages will help you achieve your goals as a modern Designer.

www.ingramcontent.com/pod-product-compliance
Lightning Source LLC
LaVergne TN
LVHW022125060326
832903LV00063B/4063